THE HEBREW LESSON

A Play

by Wolf Mankowitz

FOR AMATEUR PRODUCTION ENQUIRIES

UNITED KINGDOM AND WORLD
EXCLUDING NORTH AMERICA

plays@samuelfrench.co.uk

020 7255 4302/01

Each title is subject to availability from Samuel French,
depending upon country of performance.

For pronunciation of Yiddish, Gaelic and Hebrew
words, see Notes.

The help of Mr Sidney Lightman and
Mr Seamus Daly is gratefully acknowledged.

THE HEBREW LESSON

The large attic room of a decaying eighteenth century house in Cork.
The room has been laid out roughly as the interior of a synagogue, with
a raised platform with a piece of baluster around its centre, chairs and
benches at present disarranged around it, and a large wardrobe with an
embroidered cloth hanging on it facing us and being used as the Ark of
the Law. An elderly JEW, bearded, wearing a skull-cap and huge
praying-shawl, studies concentratedly at the lectern on the platform.
He might be praying, but actually he is learning the Irish for numbers
and certain essential phrases, translating them from his native Yiddish
into the English of the text books before him, and then into Irish. He
has lived in Cork for thirty years, and has traces of an Irish accent upon
his Yiddish English.

From the streets outside, the sounds of firing, occasional shouts, and
boots running over the cobbles to all of which he does not react.

The year: 1921. The time: very late on a mild Friday night.

JEW   Einz, zwei, drei, fier, finf, sechs, sieben, ucht, nein,
                zehn. One, two, three, four, five, six, seven, eight,
                nine, ten. Aon, dó, trí, ceathair, cúig, sé, seacht,
                ocht, naoi, deich. Penneh, schilling, fund. Yedes
                schtick kost sechs penneh, odder zwei far zehn penneh.
                A spezeeler preis. Pennies, shillings, pounds. The
                price is six pennies each, or two for tenpence, a
                special price. Pinginí, scilleaca, púint. Sé réal an
                ceann an pragas nó dá ceann ar deic pingine, pragas
                specialta. Eer kennt meer bezollen zwei penneh a vokh.
                I can collect two pence vickler. Is féidir lom da pingin

do bailiúgoluai. De zeidene shull kost drei penneh. Siz gemucht von indishen zeid. The silk scarf is threepence. It's an Indian silk scarf. Ta tri pingin ar an scairf síodac. Is scairf indíuc síodac é. Hoizen, was far a greis? Zocken, shvarts odder veiss, emessdicker boimvol, a penneh mit a halleb yedes por. Trousers, what size? Stockings, black or white, pure cotton, three halfpence a pair. Brístí, cén tómas? Stocai, dub nó bán fíor-cadás trí leitpingin peidre.

(While he studies, a MAN has entered the open attic window silently, and stands frozen, a pistol in his hand trained upon the JEW. The sounds from the street are nearer and finally disturb him.)

How can I study with such a ferkukte noise? Let innocent people sleep! Cossacks!

(He gets up to close the window. As he does so the MAN draws back into the shadows.)

(Loudly.)   Chazerim! Pigs! Mumserim! Black and brown bastards! Bithiunaigh!

MAN   (with a Cork accent)   Quiet! Call them and you are a dead man.

JEW   Who said that?

(The MAN emerges. He is very young, in nondescript clothes, his face pale, ascetic, that of a novitiate of religion or revolution.)

MAN   Close the window and keep quiet.

JEW   That's a gun?

MAN   Close it!

(The JEW shrugs, closes the window and draws a curtain.)

JEW   You're a gunman.

MAN   I am.

JEW   You kill old men?

MAN   I do not.

JEW   So, put down the gun. It can go off.

MAN   (listening)   Will you be quiet?

JEW   What should I do, sing?

MAN   I do not want to frighten you.

JEW   Who's frightened? I'm too old to be frightened. I've
           seen worse, Cossacks.   The streets ran with blood.

           (The MAN comes into the area of light from another
           lamp on the platform.)

           Tsk-tsk. You're a young man, a boy almost.

MAN   Well, we're almost a young country.   What is this place?

JEW   This is my Stebl.

MAN   What?

JEW   I am a Jew. This place is a synagogue, not the best in
           town, but at least I made it myself. A few of us like to
           keep the old style -

MAN   (suspicious)   A Jew man? Here?

JEW   (shrugs)   What can you do? We're a travelling people.

MAN   I know about you.

JEW   (curiously)   What do you know? Did you see a Jew
           before?

MAN   One came to our market.

JEW   (interested)   Oh yes? Where?

MAN   (on guard)   Why should you care?

JEW   Nothing, only if you met a market Jew I must know him.

MAN   I'm sure. You're a close lot.

JEW   What can you do? We're a small family.

           (The MAN laughs shortly with tense nervousness.)

           There's something funny?

MAN   Fat as a synagogue cat, my father used to say.

JEW   (puzzled)   A synagogue cat?

MAN   (laughs)   Yes.

JEW   Who keeps a cat in a synagogue?

MAN   Fat, you see, from the great feast of foreskins.

                (He laughs again. The JEW is a little put out.)

JEW   Personally I don't think it's very funny, but laugh if you've got something to laugh about.

MAN   I'll stay here for a while.

JEW   Welcome. Take a seat.

                (He clears a space. The MAN crosses to the door, opens it carefully, looks out, and then closes it again.)

                Yes. I know all the markets and the pedlars, the Jewish ones. It was in the West, you say? Macroom?

MAN   Never mind.

JEW   Please yourself. You're one of those revolutionary· boys?

MAN   No questions!

JEW   All right, you're a young angel of death. This is a holy house, so come in, angel. Oy, you look tired to death, angel.

MAN   (suspiciously)   Were you talking Irish before?

JEW   Dia duit! Go mairir céad bliain is go raib fice mac agus míle muc agat.

MAN   What kind of greeting is that? Twenty sons and a thousand pigs!

JEW   (proudly)   It's a little something I threw together myself. You think the customers will appreciate it? I need Irish for my business. I learnt: Dia duig. Slán leat. Slán agat. I sell goods by weekly payment. I'm a vickler. Ta fáilte rómat dom tig-se.

MAN   Gura mait agat. But twenty sons and a thousand pigs! There's nothing wrong with our old greetings. Céad mile fáilte águs bás don impíarialaí.

JEW   The first part I understand – one hundred and fifty thousand welcomes.

MAN   A hundred thousand.

JEW   All right. For you, a hundred thousand. What was the rest of it?

MAN   Death to the English!

JEW   A cholera on them, we used to say. Only then it was the
           Russian Empire. Where's all that gone? All these
           empires come down into the dust and then a little child
           walks on it.

MAN   Please God.

JEW   Now, that's a Jewish expression.

MAN   And Irish.

JEW   Why not? God is a marvellous linguist. You look pale.
           You look white as death. Poor young angel of death, sit
           down.

           (The MAN collapses into a chair, suddenly no longer on
           guard.)

MAN   I've been running all night.

JEW   I remember the feeling.

MAN   Is there anything to eat here?

JEW   It's not a restaurant, but I'll find –

MAN   Or drink?

JEW   There's the wine for the Sabbath.   (He indicates the
           wine laid out for the Friday night ceremony.)
           Take some.

MAN   Not strong drink. I'm a pioneer.

JEW   When about to die any man is a pioneer. Drink. It'll do
           you good. You can put the gun down.

           (The MAN puts the gun in his pocket, takes the bottle and
           drinks greedily from it. The JEW watches him for a
           moment, then looks at a table with the remains of a meal
           on it.)

JEW   Good. I have a piece of gefilte fish still in the bowl I
           brought up for dinner. My daughter made it.

MAN   Fish?

JEW   Gefilte. Eat. It's Friday, isn't it?

MAN   That's fish in the Jewish?

JEW   That's the best fish in any language. Here!   (He offers the bowl and a spoon.)

MAN   (doubtfully)   Hmmmm?

JEW   Eat, eat.

MAN   (tastes it carefully)   Hm!

JEW   It's good.

MAN   It's not so bad.

JEW   It's sustained the Jewish people like manna in a
thousand desert-lands.

(The MAN eats with increasing appetite. The JEW
watches him thoughtfully.)

JEW   Did you kill somebody?

MAN   I told you, no questions.

JEW   I killed a man once.

MAN   You did?

JEW   It's not so difficult. But it was a pity. He was only a
stupid peasant and drunk and poor. For him anti-semitism
was a kind of business, a pogrom was a chance to improve
his standard of living. I didn't know I was hitting him so
hard, with a poker it was. Still - what was the use of
apologising? His head was smashed in. After that I left.
We came to Cork. That was in eighteen-ninety something.
Now it's 1921. Time flies. You know something? I
thought it was New York here, because the bastard in
Lithuania who sold me the ticket told me it said New York!

(The MAN has been eating the fish ravenously, not paying
any attention to the JEW's conversation.)

Just making polite conversation. The fish is good, eh?

(The sound of a patrol car passing outside. The MAN
starts.)

MAN   I must go.

JEW   That's a good idea?

MAN   They'll search.

JEW   A Jewish house? What for? Downstairs is my daughter
and her family, and downstairs again is the old iron, the

silk scarves and the socks. In the backyard is a horse and cart and more old iron. Why should they search? Mind you, the horse is an Irishman. I call him Cuchulainn, because he's an old dog.   (He listens.)   They've gone.

MAN   (relaxes)   Your pronunciation's not bad.

JEW   Thank you. Aach! At my age I must give myself lessons again. My family for a thousand years are learning new languages, but this is ridiculous. Tá trí pingin ar an scairf síodac.

MAN   Ceannóinn é ac níl trí pingin agam.

JEW   Now, just a minute. This is a good opportunity for a conversation lesson. Duitse pragas specíalta dá pingin ar an bfíor indíac síodac scairf.

MAN   That's very good, only you should say scairf indíac síodac.

JEW   It's an impossible language. Thirty years I'm trying to learn.

MAN   Not at all. No more than yours.

JEW   Mine? Which mine? Yasik czary e ich kasaki? Vilst reden mummaloshen? What language is mine?

MAN   Say something in Jew language.

JEW   Vas fur a yolde!

MAN   What was that?

JEW   That's Yiddish. I'll read something in Hebrew.

MAN   What's the difference?

JEW   What's the difference between English and Irish?
(He opens a book and reads from a Psalm.)   'Im ech ka-chach yurushalyim tish cach yimimi.'

MAN   For God's sake!

JEW   (patiently)   'Im'.

MAN   Im is butter.

JEW   In Irish it's butter. 'Ech ka-chach' -

MAN   (curiously)   'Ech ka-chach'.

JEW   (surprised)   It's marvellous the way you make a 'ch'.

MAN   It's a sound only the English can't make. I have an old
aunt who says the Irish are descended from the ten lost
tribes.

JEW   I don't think so. They couldn't have got _so_ lost.

MAN   (suspiciously)   What do you mean?

JEW   Try again. 'Im ech'.

(The MAN slowly repeats it after him, showing a quick
ear for the language.)

You've got a good ear.

MAN   What's it mean? For you a special price, twopence.
(He laughs.)

JEW   (indignantly)   Certainly not. No business in Hebrew.
It's a holy language. It's for prayers, for psalms, for
poetry, not for selling socks. Except in Palestine.
They're growing trees there and picking oranges all in
Hebrew. A group from my village went, some boys with
long side curls and a few girls with red handkerchiefs
round their hair. And now they are speaking Hebrew the
whole time while they pick the oranges. That was
before the war.

MAN   The German war?

JEW   The Japanese.

MAN   When was there a war with them?

JEW   Sometime. I forget.

MAN   Why didn't you go yourself?

JEW   I was a married man with a family and I sell socks. I
don't grow oranges.

MAN   Oranges.

JEW   For me? What do I need it for? I'm a city man.

MAN   You city men are all alike.

(Indistinct voices from the street below. The MAN
starts.)

What am I doing talking here? Thanks for your fish and

your wine. I must be away.

(From the street below voices are heard.)

1st VOICE   You two, try the alley!

2nd VOICE   Keep both ends of the street covered!

             (The JEW and the MAN look at one another in silence.
             The MAN takes out his gun.)

MAN   Turn out the light and open the window.

JEW   Why draw attention?

MAN   Look, man, I shall have to shoot my way out. There's
             nothing else for it.

JEW   So, you'll get killed.

MAN   I'll not be the last.

JEW   You'll be the last and the first. Whoever destroys a
             single human life it's as if he has destroyed the whole
             world.

MAN   (impatiently)   I've no time for talk. Put out the light!

JEW   Just a minute.   (He takes off his praying-shawl and
             puts it on the MAN.)

MAN   What are you doing, for God's sake?

JEW   A minute, a minute! It makes you a better patriot to be
             dead?   (He opens a drawer and takes out a skull cap.)

MAN   What are you thinking about? Look, they'll never take
             me for one of yours.

JEW   Try this one. It's nice, with a silk embroidery, from
             Palestine.   (He puts the skull-cap on the MAN's
             head.)

MAN   Are you making a joke of me?

             (The JEW studies him carefully for a moment.)

             Finish now, will you? I look ridiculous.

             (Actually the MAN looks very Jewish, except for the
             gun in his hand.)

JEW   There's something wrong. Of course -   (He takes a
             prayer book, puts it in the MAN's hand and takes the

gun away.)   Now, that's perfect. Maybe you even
look Jewish. Just a minute!   (He turns the book round
the right way.)   It reads from right to left.

MAN   Give it back here!   (He grabs his gun back.)

JEW   As you like. But it spoils the whole effect.

MAN   I'll keep it hidden.

JEW   A gun under a praying shawl! It's not nice.

MAN   (grimly)   I'll try not to spoil it when I fire.

JEW   With God's help you won't fire.

MAN   You think God wants to save the lives of those bastards?

JEW   God wants us to study, that's what. Sit down! Read.
(He shows him the place in the book.)

MAN   Jesus! More lessons!

JEW   The same phrase. Try it. You never know when it'll
come in useful.

(Sounds of men nearer outside.)

MAN   (desperately)   I must get out of here.

JEW   You'll never get away. Say again. 'Im ech-kachach
yurushalayim tish cach yimini. Tidbuck leshoni
lechichi im lo ezerechi, im lo a'aleh et yurushalayim ul
rosh simchati.' Now try.

(He says the first phrase slowly in Hebrew again and the
MAN repeats it after him.)

Good, good. Again. 'Im ech-kachach yurushalayim'.

MAN   'Im ech-kachach yurushalayim'.

(There is a noise on the stairs outside as heavy boots
approach. The MAN starts up from his seat and
reaches for his gun. The JEW puts his hand on his arm.)

JEW   Quiet, quiet. Again. 'Im ech-kachach yurushalayim'.

(The door is kicked open and two BLACK AND TANS
enter.)

1st B & T   What the hell's going on in here?

JEW   Good evening to you, officer, or, strictly speaking, good morning. In either case it's good to feel that a citizen's protected no matter what time of the day or night it is.

1st B & T What's this, then? (He looks round suspiciously.)

JEW This, officer, is a place of religious worship and instruction, a synagogue. It's not much but it's all we've got.

(The 2nd BLACK AND TAN is roughly searching for arms, making a mess in doing so.)

2nd B & T Bloody Irish yid!

JEW You put your finger on it instantly, officer.

1st B & T What are you doing up at this time of night?

JEW We are religious men, officer. What have we got to do? When we do not do business we study, and when we do not study we do business.

2nd B & T Bloody yids! Come on, Charlie, there's nothing here.

1st B & T What's he, then?

2nd B & T Typical yid, ain't he?

JEW A country man, just arrived. Doesn't speak a word of our beautiful English language. (To MAN.) 'Im ech-kachach yurushalayim'. Right?

MAN 'Im ech-kachach yurushalayim'.

1st B & T What did he say?

JEW He made a blessing for you. He's a religious boy.

2nd B & T Bugger his blessing! Let's get on, Charlie.

1st B & T Just a minute. Have a look around. (Pointedly.) See if there's anything suspicious we ought to take away with us. Right?

2nd B & T (delighted) That's right. These yids have got all sorts of very suspicious gold candlesticks and all that kind of clobber, 'aven't they?

JEW You are welcome to search. Any gold candlesticks we have got we are pleased to contribute to your noble cause. These are brass. (He looks to the MAN and nods.)

MAN Im ech-kachach yurushalyim.

(The 2nd BLACK AND TAN examines the brass sticks
and throws them down disgustedly.)

JEW   My friend agrees. He says help yourself to the gold
               candlesticks.

               (The 2nd BLACK AND TAN continues opening cupboards,
               making a mess, throwing holy books and praying shawls
               out disgustedly. The MAN is barely able to suppress his
               fury at this. The JEW again restrains him with a look.)

               Im ech-kachach yurushalyim.

1st B & T   Fat as a synagogue cat. Look at him!

JEW   Chup a cholera, du mumserim! Bless you, sir!

1st B & T   Bloody unholy gabble! Come on, Tom, let's get out of
               this Jew shit-house!

               (A voice from below is heard.)

VOICE   What the bloody hell are you two doing up there? Having
               an orgy?

1st B & T   Nothing up here, Sergeant-Major. Coming right down,
               sir. Come on, Tom, for Christ's sake!

2nd B & T   Might as well take this.   (He picks up the bottle of
               wine, takes a drag and spits it out, spraying the JEW
               and the books.)   Bleedin' hell. What kind of Jew piss
               is that?

               (He tosses the bottle behind disgustedly as they both exit.
               The JEW listens a moment to the sound of the descending
               footsteps, wiping off the wine from his face.)

MAN   Bastards.

JEW   At least they appreciate the jokes your father taught you.
               (The JEW closes the door and sets about picking up the
               books and refolding the shawls. Each book as he lifts, he
               touches briefly with his lips, and wipes.)

MAN   (with self-disgust)   The dirty, filthy, stinking,
               murdering bastards! I should have shot them down.

               (He throws the cap and the shawl off furiously. The JEW
               calmly continues to tidy up.)

JEW   Sure. We would all be meat in the gutter by now. Perfect
               dignity is a dead man?

MAN   We're different from you. We fight for our dignity.

JEW   (shrugs)   Please yourself. But do me a favour,
             please, don't fight for mine. I prefer to live and
             remember.

MAN   I am prepared to die for my cause.

JEW   Well, that's brave. But from my life I can tell you that
             it's harder to live.

MAN   What's the use of talking? I must get on.

JEW   Anyway, don't feel too bad about it. You can die another
             night, if you insist.

             (A WOMAN's VOICE is heard from below.)

WOMAN'S
VOICE   Father, are you all right?

JEW   (calls)   I am all right. The lesson is going perfectly.
             (To MAN.)   Better wait another hour or two. The
             curfew will be over.

MAN   (uncomfortable)   I must thank you.

JEW   You already thanked me.

MAN   It's an odd thing to find one of you on our side.

JEW   The hunted are all on the same side.

MAN   (hesitantly)   Maybe I should tell you –

JEW   (quickly)   Don't tell me anything.

MAN   You're right.

             (There is the sound from the street below of the soldiers
             and the patrol cars leaving. The MAN and the JEW
             listen. Then there is a moment of absolute quiet.)

             They won't come back this way now.

JEW   Maybe.

MAN   I'll be going on, then.

JEW   I expect so.

             (The MAN, about to leave, hesitates and turns.)

MAN   I don't understand you people. Weren't you even angry when they threw your holy books down?

JEW   Books are just books, only the words are holy. You
             remember? 'Im ech-kachech yurushalyim'.

MAN   'Im ech-kachech yurushalyim'.

JEW   That's very good. Your accent isn't bad at all.

MAN   What does it mean?

JEW   'If I forget thee, O Jerusalem, may my right hand lose
             its cunning. May my tongue cleave to the roof of my
             mouth if I forget thee, Jerusalem. '

MAN   I know the passage well. It's in our Bible.

JEW   I'm glad to hear it. So, be careful.

MAN   I will.

JEW   Remember, God loves a live man just as much as a
             dead boy.

MAN   (smiles)   I'll remember.

JEW   Good boy. Maybe you'll be President one day. Lech
             leshalom.

MAN   Imig i síocán.

             (The MAN exits by the door. The JEW looks after him
             for a moment, then crosses to the lectern, humming to
             himself, and continues his lesson from a small book.)

             Sé sé pingin an ceann an pragas. The day is not good.
             Níl an lá go mair. The morning is not nice. Níl an
             maidin go deas. The night is very long. Tá an oice
             ana fada. Aaah!

             (He sighs deeply, suddenly very tired, and the curtain
             descends as he closes his eyes and rests his head on the
             lectern.)

NOTES AND PRONUNCIATION

(The sound represented by 'kh' is the same as 'ch' in the
Scottish 'loch' or German 'nicht'.)

Page 1   Yiddish: Eynss, tzvy, dry, fear, fineff, zecks, sibben,
ukht, nyn, tzen. Penneh, shilling, foond. Yédess
shtick kost secks penneh, odder tzvy far tzen penneh. A
spétzee'éller pryce. Eer kent mere betsóllen zvy penneh
a vōkh. Duh zýdenne shull kost dry penneh. Siz gemúkht
fon índishen zyde. Hoitzen, voss far a gryce? Zócken,
shvarts odder vyss, eméssdicker boímvoll, a penneh mit
a hálleb yédess por.

Gaelic: Āy-ūn, dhough, tree, káhir, cóo-ig, shay,
shakht, okht, nā-āy, deh. Pínginee, shíllukha, póo-int.
Shay ráyul un káy-ann un price, noo gaw kháy-ann er
deh-bíngineh, price spesheeúlta. Is fáydir lum gaw
fingin duh varlóo gŏlóo-a. Tam tree píngin er un skayrf
shée-dukh. Is skayrf indéeukh shée-dukh aye. Bréeshtée,
kāne tōce? Stuckée, duv noo bawn, feer shá-dows tree le
fíngin un pýre-eh.

Page 2   ferkukte (farkúkte) - shitty
chazerim (khazérim) - pigs
mumzerim (mumzérim) - bastards
bithiunaigh (bihóonikh) - bastards

Page 3   stebl (shteeble) - prayer room   (literally: little room)

Page 4   Diá duit, go mairir céad bliain is go raib fice mac agus
mile muc agat   (Dee-á ḡuít, guh marir káy-ud bleen is
guh rev fíheh mac óggus méela muk oggút) - Good day!
May you live for a hundred years and have twenty sons
and a thousand pigs

Diá duig, slan leat, slan agat (Dee-á ḡuít, slawn lath,
slawn oggut) - Good morning, goodbye, farewell

Ta failte romat dom tig-se (taw fóyle-he róte dum híshe)
- You are welcome to my house

Gura mait agat (górra mah óggut) - thank you

Cead mile failte romhat, agus bas don impiarulai (káyud
meela fóyle-he óggus bowss dun impéeree-ulee) - a
hundred thousand welcomes and death to the imperialist

Page 5   gefílte fish - stuffed carp or boiled, seasoned fish cakes

Page 7   Cuchulainn (coo-khóolin) - literally 'Culan's Hound'. One of the great heroes of Irish mythology, Cuchulainn when a child killed the watch dog of the Smith Culan, but made amends by undertaking to guard the house in the dog's place.

Ta tri pingin ar an scairf siodac (thaw tree fíngin er un skáy-arf shéedŭkh) - the silk scarf is threepence

Ceannoinn e ac nil tri pingin agam (kháyán-owing aye akh neel tree fíngin oggum) - I'd buy it only I've not got threepence

Duitse pragas specialta da pingin ar an bfíor indiac siodac scairf (duít-she price speshiálta gaw fíngin er un vée-ur indéeukh shéedukh scayrf) - for you a special price, twopence for the pure Indian silk scarf

Yasik czary e ich kasaki (yásick kazáree ee eech kasáki) - the language of the tsars and their Cossacks

Vilst reden mummaloshen (vilst rayden múmmaloshen) - do you want to speak Yiddish?

Vas fur a yolde (vass fur a yolder) - what an idiot

Im ech ka-chach yurushalyim tish cach yimini (eem ésh-kakhékh yeróoshalayim tíshkukh yeméenee) - If I forsake thee, O Jerusalem, may my right hand lose its cunning (Psalm 137)

Page 10	Tidbuck leshoni lechichi im lo ezerechi, im lo a'aleh et yurushaayim ul rosh simchati (tídbuck leshónee lekhéekee im lo ezkerékhee, im lo a'aléh et Yeróoshalayim ull rosh simkhátee) - may my tongue cleave to the roof of my mouth if I forget thee, O Jerusalem
Page 12	Chup a cholera, du mumserim (khup a kholléra, doo mumzérim) - catch cholera, you bastards
Page 14	Imig i siocan (ímig ee héekhawn) - go in peace
	Se se pingin an ceann an pragas (shay shay fíngin un káyun un price) - the price is sixpence each
	Nil an la go mair (neel ŭn law guh mah-uh) - the day is not good
	Nil an maidin go deas (neel ŭn vádin guh dass) - the morning is not nice
	Ta an oice ana fada (thaw ŭn ée-heh ánna ádda) - the night is very long

9 780573 095474